**For my best girl, Timberly,
my son, Anthony,
my sweet Mom (editor-in-chief),
the many family and friends I'm
blessed to have, and for
YOU!**

Special thanks to Robin Hartman for all of your creative feedback.

All rights reserved. No part of this publication may be reproduced or transmitted in any form or by any means, electronic, mechanical, photocopying, recording, or otherwise without written permission from the author. For permission requests, email the author at UNeedHim2@gmail.com.

Copyright © 2021 Melissa White. Printed in the United States of America. First Edition, 2021.

ISBN: 978-1-946467-10-2 (Paperback)

ISBN: 978-1-946467-18-8 (Hardcover)

ISBN: 978-1-946467-11-9 (eBook)

Library of Congress Control Number: 2021923023

Scripture quotations taken from the (NASB®) New American Standard Bible®, Copyright © 1960, 1971, 1977, 1995 by The Lockman Foundation. Used by permission. All rights reserved. www.lockman.org

Friends and family drawings and photos are used by permission. Any other resemblance to real persons, living or dead, except for the biblical characters represented is purely coincidental and unintentional.

The Night Before Christmas in Bethlehem

Written and Illustrated by
Melissa White

'Twas the night before Christmas many Christmases ago.
There was not yet dear Santa, or stocking, or snow.

The landscape was empty of strung lights or pine tree,

And few yet knew how special tomorrow would be.

Nestled in the hills of Judea, in the city of David,
A young couple had come a long way unaided,

You see, Mary was with Child and about to deliver!
And this barn was the best he could offer to give her.

With its bellowing animals and hay all strewn about,
There was too much at stake for them to have doubt.

The Child she delivered would someday deliver all

Who would believe in Him and answer His call.

But on this night His earthly life would begin. The promised Messiah, our redemption from sin.

Once He was born, she wrapped Him up tight
And laid Him in a manger—a wonderful sight!
The North Star was marking this beautiful event
Shining brightly over the majestic gift God had sent.

Just over the hills a short distance from there
Some shepherds were guarding their sheep with great care.

When what in the sky did suddenly appear
But a whole host of angels announcing Jesus was here!

Then they told everyone they met what the angels had said.
And soon the Good News of Jesus had spread.

This promise of Hope is still reaching us today,
That Jesus, our Friend, hears us when we pray.

But there was one
who was angry to learn
That this special baby
had just been born.

Herod worried that Jesus
would take his
place as king
And refused the love
that He could bring.

But they knew it was a trick and left another way
After they had visited Jesus one day.

They gave Him frankincense, myrrh, and gold,
And kept His secret whereabouts untold.

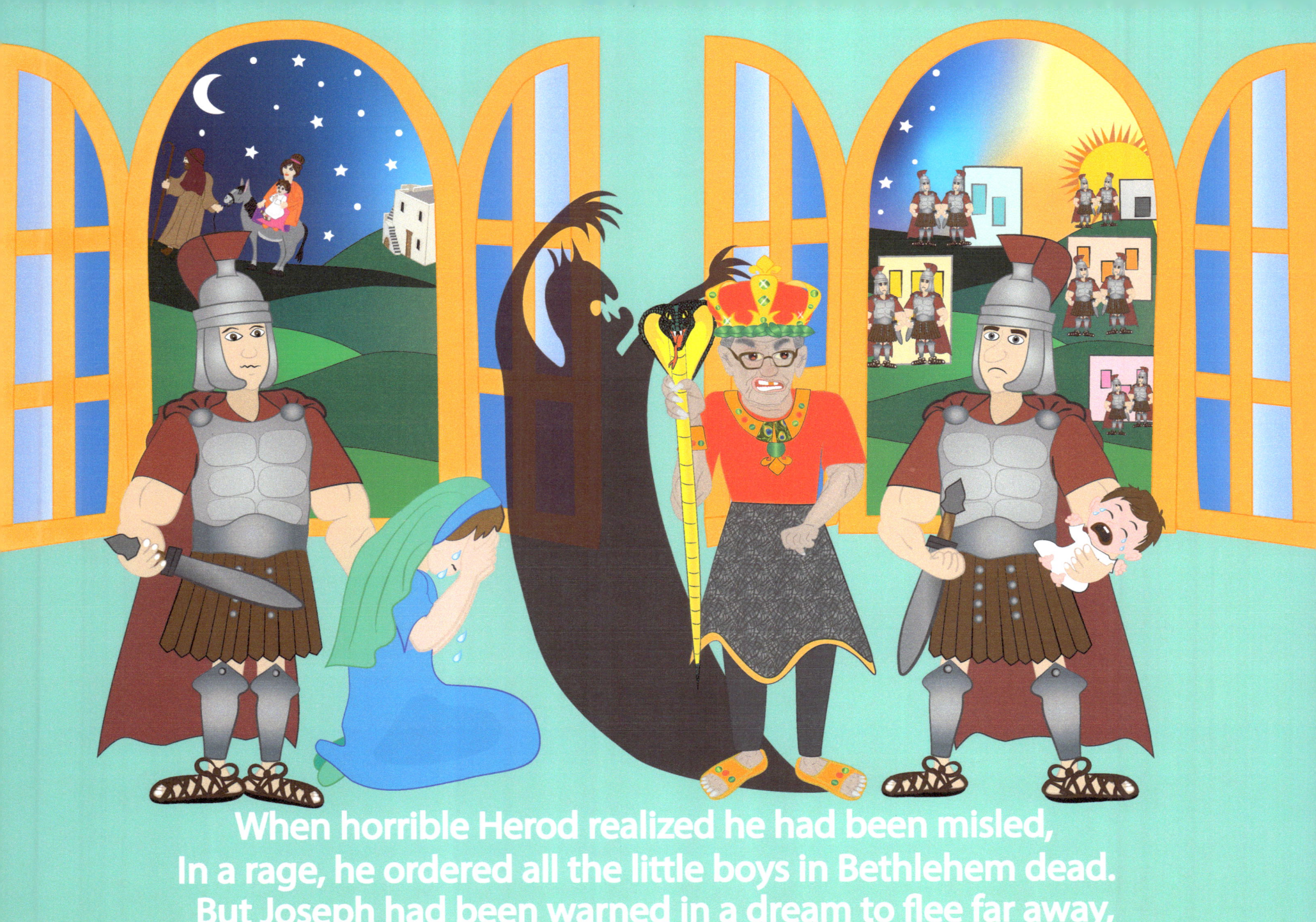

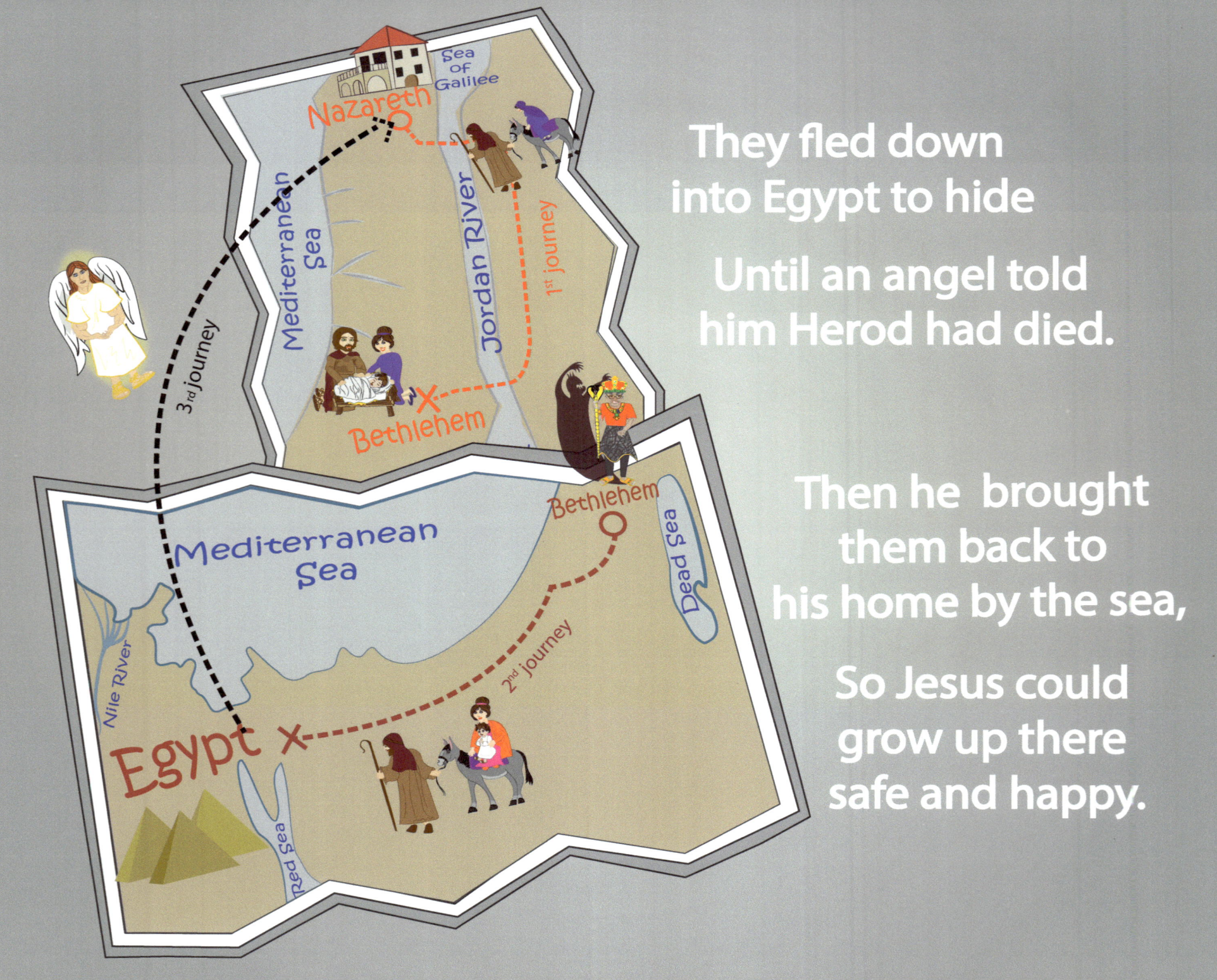

We're busy with Santa, elves, visits, and calls,
But EVER in the hustle and bustle of it all,
May we be like the shepherds and three wise men
And make time to praise and adore Him once again!

Merry CHRISTmas!

Dear Reader:

Jesus was born into the world as a special and beautiful baby on that first Christmas just like you and I were on our birthdays. He came at the exact time that Father God planned for Him to come, just like you and I came at the exact time Father God planned for us to come.

Before He was born to Mary and Joseph, Jesus lived in Heaven with Father God and the Holy Spirit as part of God's team. But Heaven had lost part of its team when satan, God's most glorious angel, decided to try to overtake God and had to be cast out of Heaven down to earth.

Ever since he lost his glory, satan has been causing trouble here, just like you see in the pages of the story. (You can see him trying to influence Herod and make the world a sad and scary place.) The very reason Jesus came to earth was to help us overcome him and live better lives.

Just like Joseph had God's help so many times in the story—the way God would lead him out of danger and protect him—God wants to help us too. We can pray **any time, anywhere**, about **anything** and receive His help in our lives. We can pray out loud or with just a whisper, and He'll hear us. The Bible promises that He will have His angels protect us and help us just like He did for Joseph and Mary. Here is one such prayer:

Father God, Holy Spirit, and Jesus, please help me today. Please protect me and guide me as I go through this day. Please give me the things that I need and teach me more about You. Please help me to make good choices and honor You today also. I want to walk with You every day. Thank You! In Jesus' Name. Amen.

Jesus is the best friend we can ever have! He loves us so much—enough to leave Heaven and come here to help us. There is a lot more to His story that happened after He grew up in Nazareth. I hope you read more about Him in the pages of your Bible or in my next book.

Your friend,
Melissa

Jesus' Birth Foretold:

Now in the sixth month the angel Gabriel was sent from God to a city in Galilee called Nazareth, to a virgin engaged to a man whose name was Joseph, of the descendants of David; and the virgin's name was Mary. And coming in, he said to her, "Greetings, favored one! The Lord is with you." But she was very perplexed at this statement, and kept pondering what kind of salutation this was. The angel said to her, "Do not be afraid, Mary; for you have found favor with God. And behold, you will conceive in your womb and bear a son, and you shall name Him Jesus. He will be great and will be called the Son of the Most High; and the Lord God will give Him the throne of His father David; and He will reign over the house of Jacob forever, and His kingdom will have no end." Mary said to the angel, "How can this be, since I am a virgin?" The angel answered and said to her, "The Holy Spirit will come upon you, and the power of the Most High will overshadow you; and for that reason the holy Child shall be called the Son of God."...And Mary said, "Behold, the bondslave of the Lord; may it be done to me according to your word." And the angel departed from her.
Luke 1:26-35, 38 NAS

Jesus' Birth in Bethlehem:

Now in those days a decree went out from Caesar Augustus, that a census be taken of all the inhabited earth. This was the first census taken while Quirinius was governor of Syria. And everyone was on his way to register for the census, each to his own city. Joseph also went up from Galilee, from the city of Nazareth, to Judea, to the city of David which is called Bethlehem, because he was of the house and family of David, in order to register along with Mary, who was engaged to him, and was with child. While they were there, the days were completed for her to give birth. And she gave birth to her firstborn son; and she wrapped Him in cloths, and laid him in a manger, because there was no room for them in the inn. In the same region there were some shepherds staying out in the fields and keeping watch over their flock by night. And an angel of the Lord suddenly stood before them, and the glory of the Lord shone around them; and they were terribly frightened. But the angel said to them, "Do not be afraid; for behold, I bring good news of great joy which will be for all the people; for today in the city of David there has been born for you a Savior, who is Christ the Lord. This will be a sign for you: you will find a baby wrapped in cloths and lying in a manger." And suddenly there appeared with the angel a multitude of the heavenly host praising God and saying, "Glory to God in the highest, and on earth peace among men with whom He is pleased." When the angels had gone away from them into heaven, the shepherds began saying to one another, "Let us go straight to Bethlehem then, and see this thing that has happened which the Lord has made known to us." So they came in a hurry and found their way to Mary and Joseph, and the baby as He lay in the manger. When they had seen this, they made known the statement which had been told them about the Child. And all who heard it wondered at the things which were told them by the shepherds. *Luke 2:1-18 NAS*

The Visit of the Magi:

Now after Jesus was born in Bethlehem of Judea in the days of Herod the king, magi from the east arrived in Jerusalem, saying "Where is He who has been born King of the Jews? For we saw His star in the east and have come to worship Him." When Herod the king heard of this, he was troubled, and all Jerusalem with him. Gathering together all the chief priests and scribes of the people, he inquired of them where the Messiah was to be born. They said to him, "In Bethlehem of Judea; for this is what has been written by the prophet: AND YOU, BETHLEHEM, LAND OF JUDAH, ARE BY NO MEANS LEAST AMONG THE LEADERS OF JUDAH; FOR OUT OF YOU SHALL COME FORTH A RULER WHO WILL SHEPHERD MY PEOPLE ISRAEL." Then Herod secretly called the magi and determined from them the exact time the star appeared. And he sent them to Bethlehem and said, "Go and search carefully for the Child; and when you have found Him, report to me, so that I too may come and worship Him." After hearing the king, they went their way; and the star, which they had seen in the east, went on before them until it came and stood over the place where the Child was. When they saw the star, they rejoiced exceedingly with great joy. After coming into the house, they saw the Child with Mary His mother; and they fell to the ground and worshipped Him. Then, opening their treasures, they presented to Him gifts of gold, frankincense, and myrrh. And having been warned by God in a dream not to return to Herod, the magi left for their own country by another way. *Matthew 2:1-12 NAS*

The Flight to Egypt:

Now when they had gone, behold, an angel of the Lord appeared to Joseph in a dream and said, "Get up! Take the Child and His mother and flee to Egypt, and remain there until I tell you; for Herod is going to search for the Child to destroy Him." So Joseph got up and took the Child and His mother while it was still night, and left for Egypt. He remained there until the death of Herod. *Matthew 2:13-15 NAS*

Herod Slaughters Babies:

Then when Herod saw that he had been tricked by the magi, he became very enraged, and sent and slew all the male children who were in Bethlehem and all its vicinity, from two years old and under, according to the time which he had determined from the magi. Then what had been spoken through Jeremiah the prophet was fulfilled: "A VOICE WAS HEARD IN RAMAH, WEEPING AND GREAT MOURNING, RACHEL WEEPING FOR HER CHILDREN; AND SHE REFUSED TO BE COMFORTED, BECAUSE THEY WERE NO MORE." But when Herod died, behold, an angel of the Lord appeared in a dream to Joseph in Egypt, and said, "Get up, take the Child and His mother, and go into the land of Israel; for those who sought the Child's life are dead." So Joseph got up, took the Child and His mother, and came into the land of Israel. But when he heard that Archelaus was reigning over Judea in place of his father, Herod, he was afraid to go there. Then after being warned by God in a dream, he left for the regions of Galilee, and came and lived in a city called Nazareth. *Matthew 2:16-23 NAS*

www.ingramcontent.com/pod-product-compliance
Lightning Source LLC
Chambersburg PA
CBHW042110090526

44592CB00004B/71